JESUS LEADERSHIP

Master One Simple Habit to Thrive in Life, Love and Leadership

A 7-Week Training Journal

Stephen Shoff

Jesus Leadership: Master One Simple Habit to Thrive in Life, Love and Leadership

Printed in the United States of America.

ISBN: 978-1-948450-83-6.

Cover design by Stephen Shoff. Interior layout by Toney Mulhollan.

Illumination Publishers titles may be purchased in bulk for classroom instruction, business, fund-raising, or sales promotional use. For information, please email paul.ipibooks@me.com.

Illumination Publishers cares deeply about using renewable resources and uses recycled paper whenever possible.

About the author: Stephen J. Shoff is dedicated to helping people, teams and communities thrive. He's witnessed the transformational power of Jesus' teaching and training around the world having served extensively in ministry, business and mission-work in the US and Japan. He and his wife Sue live in Vermont.

Illumination Publishers International
www.ipibooks.com
6010 Pinecreek Ridge Court
Spring, Texas 77379-2513

JESUS IS REVOLUTIONARY

He grew up in the neighborhood, made friends, studied hard, worked a construction job – then went on to change the world joyfully, overcoming extreme adversity and redefining greatness forever. He had a radical dream and the courage to make it happen. His wisdom and influence continue to sweep through history, inspiring every aspect of human existence. And he was a small group leader. Imagine for a moment that you are on Jesus' training team. What do you see? How do you feel? What are you learning? How are you growing? What will you go and do? Those who are trained become like their teacher. So it was for the Twelve – so it will be for us. *Let's devote ourselves to learning from Jesus in order to become more like him and so carry forth his revolution of love.*

One Simple Revolutionary Habit: Train with Jesus every day

Hear + Practice = Thrive

"Therefore everyone who hears these words of mine and puts them into practice is like a wise man who built his house on the rock. The rain came down, the streams rose, and the winds blew and beat against that house; yet it did not fall, because it had its foundation on the rock."

–Jesus (Matthew 7:24–25)

CONTENTS

CONTENTS

ABOUT THIS REVOLUTION

This revolution will give you the tools to change yourself and change the world. If you are passionate about making your life, love and leadership count, this is your revolution.

Jesus is your expert teacher-trainer-coach. Train to be your best with the greatest teacher and coach in history. Jesus' life was characterized by great faith, hope and love, and yours can be too.

The Gospels are the primary training manuals. The four New Testament Gospels (Matthew, Mark, Luke and John) are packed with eyewitness accounts of unforgettable scenarios in which Jesus led and trained ordinary people to live extraordinary lives – real-life case studies of Jesus in action and his principles in practice. Get your Bible out and get ready to train with the best.

This revolution guarantees results. Jesus said that when we hear his words and put them into practice, we can overcome any challenge to build lives that are healthy and strong for the long haul.

This revolution requires daily practice to form healthy habits. Jesus emphasized the importance of a fundamental habit: hearing and practicing his words every day.

This revolution will develop your whole character. All of us have four distinct but integrated parts of our character: mind/mental/thinking, heart/emotional/feeling, soul/spiritual/believing and body/physical/doing. Jesus trains each part in balance.

This revolution is an inside-out approach to personal development. Jesus taught that it's who we are on the inside that determines our results on the outside. This course starts with your core character leadership – you leading *you* well – and then works outward toward leading others well by building strong one-another relationships, growing your team, effectively leading in the neighborhood and then training other leaders. Healthy leadership of others starts with healthy leadership of self.

HOW TO USE THIS JOURNAL

Step #1 – ***Plan and commit to study and write in this journal every day for seven weeks.*** Know this: even a quick interaction with Jesus can be revolutionary – just ask Peter, the Samaritan woman, Legion, the centurion, blind Bartimaeus, Zacchaeus the tax collector, Jairus' daughter, Mary Magdalene, Nicodemus the Pharisee, the thief on the cross and billions of others throughout history. Jesus said, *"Everyone who hears these words of mine and puts them into practice is like a wise man who built his house on the rock"* (Matthew 7:24). These daily guided workout-devotionals are designed to help you build the hear-and-practice habit and to grow in Christ in the focus area of the week. A suggested format is: Pray to prepare yourself to learn. Then read that day's devotional and scriptures for a few minutes. Next, write down your insights – what you're "hearing." Then spend a few minutes planning your practice. Pray some more. Now go and grow!

Step #2 – ***Ask someone to partner with you in your training. Training with a partner is much more effective than training alone.*** Ideally, your partner will be someone you can talk with regularly – a trusting relationship in which you support, challenge, encourage and believe in one another. Some great questions to ask each another and discuss: "What have you been hearing? How have you been practicing? What are you learning? What are your dreams and goals? How can I support you? How can we help one another?"

Step #3 – ***Push yourself every day to take two simple yet revolutionary action steps.*** 1) Hear Jesus' words to YOU and 2) practice his words to YOU. When you do this, forming this essential habit in your daily life, you will grow and succeed – Jesus himself guarantees it! (Matthew 7:24–27, Luke 6:46–49, James 1:22–25).

Step #4 – ***Enjoy the process: get into it, have fun, be wholehearted, make every effort!*** Growth takes time, but when we're growing, we experience joy. Remember, you're building your house on the Rock – to endure, flourish and prosper into eternity!

REVOLUTION KICK-START

Change is powered by both inspiration and desperation – desire, hope and hunger. Take a few moments to write down a few things you're thankful for and the dreams of growth that energize you.

First, Give Thanks:

Looking up to heaven, he gave thanks. – Matthew 14:19

Growth Dreams and Visions:

Jesus grew in wisdom and stature, and in favor with God and man. – Luke 2:52

Week One

JESUS: LEADER

Love in Action

7 Ways Jesus Lived Love in Action:

1. **BEST FRIEND**
2. **STREET CHAMPION**
3. **ROCK STAR**
4. **LIFE DOCTOR**
5. **HUMBLE SLAVE**
6. **PIONEER OF POSSIBLE**
7. **MASTER & COMMANDER**

Jesus is history's most successful human – and we get to learn from him. He invites each of us to train with him and be developed by him, and so become like him in heart, soul, mind and strength. But first we must get to know him, learning that we can trust him and follow him with our whole lives.

BEST FRIEND

"Greater love has no one than this: to he lay down one's life for one's friends." (John 15:13)

Jesus summed up success in life in one word: love (Mark 12:28–31, Matthew 22:37–40, John 13:34–35). Live a life of love and you will succeed – emotionally, physically, mentally and spiritually – guaranteed. Love God. Love one another. Love your neighbor as yourself. Love never fails. God is love. Jesus came to inspire us, to show us, to teach us the way of love. He is a true friend. He has great faith, hope and love for each one of us. He's family; he grew up in the neighborhood. Jesus sympathizes with our weaknesses; he knows our fears, struggles, temptations and challenges – and still has crazy-big vision for us. He died for us. He celebrates our dreams, strengths, successes and accomplishments. Jesus laughed, cried, hung out, partied, dreamed, worked, played, suffered and died side by side with us. Read **John 2:1–13** and **Luke 23:26–43**. What stands out to you about Jesus' attitude toward people? Write down your insights. What do you hear from these accounts about Jesus' attitude toward you? How has he been a best friend to you – genuinely loved you? Today, take some time to remember and thank him for love. What are you hearing? How will you practice? Pray.

Today: Hear + Practice:

Because he himself suffered when he was tempted, he is able to help those who are being tempted. (Hebrews 2:18)

STREET CHAMPION

"Zeal for your house will consume me." (John 2:17)

Jesus was a street fighter – a champion of honor for God and all people. He fought the important fights with great faith, valiant zeal and inspiring integrity, and won. Read **John 2:12–22**. What do you learn about Jesus from this account? Often when people heard Jesus speak or saw him in action they were "amazed," "astonished" and "delighted" (Matthew 13:54, Mark 1:22, Luke 20:26, Luke 13:17). Why does Jesus have this effect on us? Read **Luke 7:11–17**. How did Jesus use his power to tenderly love this mourning mom and her son? How has he used his power to fight for you? Today, practice knowing Jesus as the faith-fierce, compassionate and street-smart fighter that he is. Live today in awe, inspired by your champion. Pray.

Today: Hear + Practice:

His heart went out to her and he said, "Don't cry." (Luke 7:13)

ROCK STAR

"Like a wise man who built his house on the rock..." (Matthew 7:24)

Jesus is trustworthy and true, inspirational and visionary, of strong character and charismatic, both the eternal Rock and the bright Morning Star. His life and teachings are rooted in ethical principles and practices – inspired and energized by idealistic dreams, love relationships and extraordinary faith. He spoke to fundamental human longings, needs and aspirations. He did astounding miracles, gave hope to the hurting, healed the sick and raised the dead. Take a few minutes to read **Matthew 5:1–16,** the beginning of the Sermon on the Mount. This master class is one of the most influential in human history. As you read it, what are you hearing from Jesus about your life's value and purpose? Jesus is trying to help you to be eternally successful. Write down your thoughts. How will you practice just one principle from the Sermon on the Mount today? Pray.

Today: Hear + Practice:

"You are the light of the world." (Matthew 5:14)

LIFE DOCTOR

"It is not the healthy who need a doctor, but the sick." (Mark 2:17)

Sin is unhealthy and makes us sick emotionally, spiritually, mentally and physically. Jesus guides us to health in our whole life – heart, soul, mind and body. He inspires and trains us from the inside out. He knows how we're made and what we're made for. He teaches real-life solutions to real-life problems. Jesus got involved with everyone – religious, pagan, rich, poor, sick, sinners, saints, rulers and regular folk. With grace and truth, power and compassion, he teaches us how to thrive – to live life to the full (John 10:10). Jesus is willing to get messy and bloody to make us healthy and whole. Read **Mark 2:1–17.** What are you hearing about who Jesus is and how he relates to us? Note your insights. How has he helped you to live well? Today, practice allowing Jesus to be your personal life doctor. Write down your thoughts and plans. Pray.

Today: Hear + Practice:

In him was life, and that life was the light of all mankind. (John 1:4)

HUMBLE SLAVE

"Whoever wants to become great among you must be your servant, and whoever wants to be first must be slave of all." (Mark 10:43–44)

Jesus believes that every one of us is incredibly valuable and uniquely awesome. He sees our massive potential for greatness and weeps when we waste it (Luke 19:41). He knows that God created each of us for greatness – to flourish and multiply (Genesis 1:26–31). He considers our dignity, our salvation, our eternal lives and our souls worth becoming a slave and dying for. Amazing! Jesus wants to help you discover and develop your best. Now read and think about **Mark 10:35–45**. As you consider this passage, what stands out to you? What is so different about Jesus' description of strong leadership compared to most definitions? **Read John 19:16–37**. How did Jesus make himself your humble slave? How will you practice humility and service of others today? Note your insights and plans. Pray.

Today: Hear + Practice:

"Take my yoke upon you and learn from me, for I am gentle and humble in heart." (Matthew 11:29)

REVOLUTION

PIONEER OF POSSIBLE

"With man this is impossible, but with God all things are possible." (Matthew 19:26)

Jesus was confident in God and deeply connected to him in heart, soul, mind and body. He trusted him completely. Even in the worst darkness, he believed in God's love, power and wisdom for victory – making him our pioneer of possible (Hebrews 12). Think about a pressure-packed situation that you've experienced recently. How did you respond in the moment? Consider your mental, emotional, spiritual and physical response. Did you see with eyes of faith? Did you respond with faithful emotions? Did you trust God to make the impossible, possible? Now read **Mark 9:2–32**. What do you learn about the power of God? In these challenging situations, how did Jesus' attitude and faith compare to that of those around him? What does Jesus say is the relationship between prayer and the possible? How has Jesus paved the way for possible in your life? Take a moment to thank him for his faithful leadership. Consider how Jesus is training you to face your challenges differently. Now pray and go pioneer some possible!

Extra-Strength Exercise: Write down a few outrageous, fun, radical, "impossible" dreams that Jesus is inspiring in your life.

Today: Hear + Practice:

"If you have faith...nothing will be impossible for you."
(Matthew 17:20)

MASTER & COMMANDER

"All authority in heaven and on earth has been given to me." (Matthew 28:18)

Many people have held high positions of stature and achieved amazing feats. Jesus surpasses them all. He's the only human ever who predicted his death and resurrection in detail (Matthew 17:9, Matthew 17:22–23, Matthew 20:17–19, Matthew 26:1–2) and then did it – eye-witnessed by hundreds of ordinary people just like us. During his life on earth, Jesus demonstrated dominion over nature, disease, money, death, demons, angels and more – uniquely proving his ultimate power and authority. Read Matthew 28:1–20. What are you hearing about Jesus' role in the universe and, more importantly, in your personal life? How has he used his power and authority to benefit you? How will you trust his power and authority in your life today? Write it down. Now pray and go make disciples of all nations – the Master and Commander is with you!

Extra-Strength Exercise: The word "obey" comes from the Latin ob audire, meaning "to attentively listen with the intent to practice." Talk to God about your willingness or hesitation "to obey everything" Jesus commanded. Open your heart to learning to trust and obey Jesus even when it's difficult – it's to your benefit.

Today: Hear + Practice:

"This is my Son, whom I love; with him I am well pleased. Listen to him!" (Matthew 17:5)

JESUS: LEADER WORKSHEET

Successful training requires commitment and focus. Jesus is wholeheartedly committed to you and your healthy growth. Now he's asking you to fully commit to him to be "fully trained":

I. What I most admire about Jesus:

II. What I most want to learn from Jesus (my training focus):

III. My training commitment:

"The student is not above the teacher, but everyone who is fully trained will become like their teacher." (Luke 6:40)

WEEKLY TRAINING REVIEW

Effective training is intentional. It's vitally important to consistently review and reflect upon what we're learning in order to make solid commitments and clear plans for progress. Then as we partner with God each day in prayer (Luke 5:16) we will become more and more like Jesus.

I. My main "Hear + Practice" takeaways from this past week:

II. My training dreams, commitments, plans and prayers:

"...like a man building a house, who dug down deep and laid the foundation on rock." (Luke 6:48)

Week Two

SELF-LEADERSHIP

Love God

7 Passions of Personal Growth:

1. **GOOD TREE**
2. **LOVE GOD**
3. **CULTIVATE GREAT**
4. **DAILY MISSION**
5. **TAKE ACTION**
6. **BOUNCEBACKABILITY**
7. **REST & REJUVENATE**

Jesus was passionate about his life. He understood that global revolution is powered by personal revolution. To change the world, we must first change ourselves. Jesus took full responsibility for his own heart, soul, mind and body before God. Then he went confidently on his mission, doing whatever it took to finish.

GOOD TREE

"Make a tree good and its fruit will be good." (Matthew 12:33)

God designed and created each of us for extraordinary abundance (Genesis 1:28). But the challenges of life and the deceitfulness of sin can tempt us to close down, go dark, push love away and harden our hearts – only to settle for a lonely and barren existence. Don't go there; that's no way to live! Especially when Jesus paid the ultimate price to show us the way to abundant life (John 10:10), where God's seeds of greatness thrive. Jesus is calling each of us to trust him – to open our eyes to see, our ears to hear and our hearts to understand. He wants to help us make the tree good. Read **Matthew 12:33–35** and **Matthew 13:1–23**. What do you hear Jesus saying to you in this passage? How can you make the tree good? Which of the four soils best describes you at this time in your life? Why? Write down your insights. Today, talk to God and to trustworthy people to examine yourself and receive wise feedback about your heart, what you have "stored up" and your response to God's word. Open up to God – take responsibility for yourself and the growth of his words in your life. Today, decide to be blessed, to be the good soil, to become the "good tree" to "produce a crop" – and put together a practical plan for your personal growth. Pray.

Today: Hear + Practice:

"Those with a noble and good heart, who hear the word, retain it, and by persevering produce a crop." (Luke 8:15)

LOVE GOD

"Love the Lord your God with all your heart and with all your soul and with all your mind and with all your strength." (Mark 12:30)

Loving God involves both taking responsibility *and* surrendering to him our whole heart, soul, mind and body. Our love connection to God is our most important life connection. It changes us for good and empowers us to change our world. Our relationship with God connects us to the nourishing spiritual source of abundant life. It motivates us to persevere in our love for others (2 Corinthians 5:14–15) – to please God with our best – because God gives us his best (John 3:16). Jesus taught that everything good in life springs from loving God; all other commands and promises of God hang on this one (Matthew 22:37–40). Loving and trusting God is the key to a healthy, thriving life (Jeremiah 17:5–8). Jesus was a dearly loved son (Luke 3:22) who knew and relied on God's love (John 5:20). It empowered him to live a faith-filled life of love (Ephesians 5:1–2) and to entrust himself fully to his Father's will (Matthew 26:36–46). This deep bond strengthened Jesus to start and finish his work of laying down his life for us (John 10:17, John 19:30). Read **John 13:1–5** and **John 15:1–17**. How did Jesus' love relationship with God affect how he lived? What is Jesus teaching you about loving God? How will you practice it today?

Today: Hear + Practice:

And a voice came from heaven: "You are my Son, whom I love; with you I am well pleased." (Mark 1:11)

CULTIVATE GREAT

But Jesus often withdrew to lonely places and prayed. (Luke 5:16)

You were created for greatness. You are not a mistake – far from it. God created you for a reason, on purpose, with a unique calling and cross to bear – a voice. You have a special combination of talents, opportunities and gifts with which to serve and inspire humanity (Genesis 1:26, 4:20–22, Romans 12:6, Mark 10:45). Jesus wants to help us find and live our voice with bold confidence. Often, we can discover our voice – our calling – at the intersection of what we love to do, what we're good at and what serves others. Jesus realized his calling early in life. He knew where he had come from and where he was going (John 13:3). He was humble yet clear and confident about his identity. In the Gospels, he made over twenty powerful "I am" statements. However, even Jesus had to struggle to understand and fully embrace his authentic, God-given voice (Hebrews 5:7–10). Only then could he grow into the man he became (Luke 2:40, 52, 4:18–21) and step up to the challenges ahead. Read and think about Luke 4:1–19. In this passage, how do you see Jesus fighting to connect with God's truth – to understand, train and prepare to fulfill his life's mission? What do you hear God saying to you about cultivating the greatness you were created for? Pray.

Extra-Strength Exercise: Think about a few passages of Scripture that resonate deeply with your spirit – those that inspire the best in you. Now read John 1:19–23. What scripture did John the Baptist identify with. What was his voice? What's yours?

Today: Hear + Practice:

"What do you say about yourself?" John replied in the words of Isaiah the prophet, "I am the voice..." (John 1:22–23)

DAILY MISSION

"In any case, I must press on today and tomorrow and the next day – for surely no prophet can die outside Jerusalem!" (Luke 13:33)

Our mission, if we will accept it, is to love God, one another and our neighbor *in the way that only we uniquely can.* Here's some really good news: God feels about you the same way he does about Jesus – he loves you, thinks you're awesome and has a great vision for your life. Jesus said, "I am the light of the world" (John 8:12), but he also said, "You are the light of the world" (Matthew 5:14). You, like Jesus, were created with a God-given destiny, an important mission, a reason to live. So you MUST keep going to the finish (John 19:30). Your God, your family, your friends, your team – your world – are counting on you! And we will go to the ends of the earth for a mission of love that matters to us. But know this: your mission will require everything from you – love with all your heart, soul, mind and strength, real-life sacrifice, every effort to take up your cross and deny yourself and lesser things – every day. Read **Luke 3:21–22, Luke 4:18–21, Luke 9:34–35, Luke 19:41–42, Luke 23:44–46** and **Luke 24:36–44.** How did God feel about Jesus? What was God's important mission for him? Did he complete it? Now consider how God feels about you and what his mission is for your life – will you complete it? Listen to Jesus for insight. What are you hearing? Write it down. How can you step out in faith today to internalize, practice and develop God's special mission of love for you? Dedicate yourself to finishing God's dream for you – practice your visionary mission every day, keep moving forward – and inspire your world! Pray.

Today: Hear + Practice:

"Whoever wants to be my disciple must deny themselves and take up their cross daily and follow me." (Luke 9:23)

REVOLUTION

TAKE ACTION

"I will keep on driving out demons and healing people today and tomorrow, and on the third day I will reach my goal." (Luke 13:32)

To rise from the dead and save the world is a crazy dream, but Jesus did it. Jesus was a man of decisive action – humble and hungry, focused and determined, fueled by both inspiration and desperation – with high standards of excellence. He never made excuses, never played the victim or the fool. He didn't procrastinate, shift blame or succumb to self-pity. He faced and embraced the truth. He took total responsibility for himself, his relationships, his work and completing his mission (John 5:36). Jesus taught that taking personal responsibility builds in us a deepening sense of strength, joy and freedom. Read **Luke 13:22–35**. Even in difficult circumstances, what did Jesus expect of himself? Now read **John 5:1–16**. What did Jesus expect of this man at the pool? How was this man giving in to excuses and self-pity? Now consider the excuses you tend to make. Examine yourself – consider the areas of your life where Jesus is saying to you, "Get up! Pick up your mat and walk." Write down a few of your goals and state them in the affirmative: "I will (accomplish my goal)." Now take action. Go confidently in the direction of your goals. You are great; now be great. Do your very best and trust God with the rest. Pray and play!

Extra-Strength Exercise: Write down a personal P.U.S.H (Practice Until Success Happens) goal – a big, scary, exciting goal that you really care about – with a firm deadline. Now take massive, passionate action toward accomplishing that goal.

Today: Hear + Practice:

"Get up! Pick up your mat and walk." (John 5:8)

REVOLUTION

BOUNCEBACKABILITY

"Cheer up! On your feet! He's calling you." (Mark 10:49)

We all stumble and fall, but we don't have to stay down. Life rewards grit, resilience and perseverance – "bouncebackability" (Luke 8:15, Romans 5:4, 1 Timothy 4:16, Hebrews 10:36, James 1:4, James 5:11, Revelation 2:2). We all love comeback stories – so live one. Make your trials your triumphs, your mess your message, your tests your testimony, your pain someone else's gain. Don't get down and depressed, instead get "down and determined"! This practice is called repentance. To repent is to forcefully change from unhealthy ways to healthy ways. At the start, to be born again, we repented and were baptized (John 3:3–7, Acts 2:38). But repentance is not just a one-time act – it's a daily way of life. Sometimes we just need to get mad at mediocrity, alarmed with apathy, indignant with idleness, ticked off at temptation, say "No more; this ends today; enough!" – and bounce back! And while not easy, repentance is healthy, constructive and brings refreshing (Acts 3:19, 2 Corinthians 7:8–11). Jesus is the repentance and turnaround expert – the master of overcoming the odds with faith, of turning lemons into lemonade. Read **Mark 10:46–52** and **Mark 5:1–20.** How did Jesus respond to these guys? How did Bartimaeus and Legion bounce back and make something good out of their difficult circumstances? How did they repent and believe the good news? How can you? Cheer up! On your feet! Jesus is calling you.

Today: Hear + Practice:

"Repent and believe the good news." (Mark 1:15)

REST & REJUVENATE

Jesus was in the stern, sleeping on a cushion. (Mark 4:38)

Real rest, regular rejuvenation, peaceful sleep and deep recovery are just as important to our growth as diligence, activity, industry and hard work. Even God rested from his labor for a whole day! (Genesis 2:2). And while Jesus was extremely hardworking, he was also careful to rejuvenate (Luke 21:37, John 4:6, Luke 5:16, Matthew 11:28–29). He was humble about his need for rest. Read **Mark 4:35–41**. What do you notice about Jesus' calm and faith compared to the fear and fatigue of the apostles? Rest, vibrant faith and exuberant joy go together. However, the fragile feeling of happiness can be fleeting, because happiness is based on "happenings" – circumstances often beyond our control. Joy is much more stable because it's based on the unchanging love, power and providence of God. Read **Luke 10:17–24.** How did Jesus stay joyful? How did his soul find rest in God? (Psalm 62:1). What do you hear Jesus teaching you about enjoying real, relaxing, rejuvenating, refreshing, rewarding rest? Write down your insights and thoughts. Get creative – make rest and rejuvenation a central part of your daily and weekly schedule. Pray.

Today: Hear + Practice:

"For my yoke is easy and my burden is light." (Matthew 11:30)

SELF-LEADERSHIP WORKSHEET

Jesus was purposeful and passionate about his personal growth (Luke 2:40–52, Luke 13:31–35). And he's just as excited about helping you with yours (Mark 1:17, Matthew 11:28–30). Practice every day with Jesus, and your growth is guaranteed (Matthew 12:33, Luke 9:23).

I. My personal dreams and goals:

II. How I must grow to realize my dreams and goals:

III. How I am training with Jesus every day to grow:

IV. Why my dreams and goals are important:

"I will reach my goal... In any case, I must keep going."
(Luke 13:32–33 NIV 1984)

WEEKLY TRAINING REVIEW

Review and reflect upon what you've learned this week and make solid commitments and clear plans for progress. Then partner with God each day in prayer to become more and more like Jesus (Luke 5:16).

I. My main "Hear + Practice" takeaways from this past week:

II. My training dreams, commitments, plans and prayers:

"...like a man building a house, who dug down deep and laid the foundation on rock." (Luke 6:48)

Week Three

ONE-ANOTHER LEADERSHIP

Love One Another

7 Basics of Building Friendships:

1. **MUTUALITY**
2. **RESPECT**
3. **GRACE & TRUTH**
4. **VULNERABILITY**
5. **CHARACTER**
6. **CONVERSATION**
7. **FORGIVENESS**

Humans grow strong when rooted in healthy, mutual love relationships. Jesus taught the importance of loving one another and showed us how to do it well. By this all will know that Jesus trained you. The quality of our relationships determines the quality of our lives.

MUTUALITY

"As I have loved you, so you must love one another." (John 13:34)

One-another relationships are dynamic, interdependent relationships built on mutual respect, influence, service, encouragement (Romans 1:12) and trust. Jesus said that we need relationships like this to live well (John 13:34–35, Romans 12:10, Galatians 5:13–14, Ephesians 4:32, Colossians 3:16, James 5:16). Love is action. Love sometimes causes great joy, sometimes pain – but always strength. Jesus' love – agape love – is sacrificial love in sincere service of others. Jesus loved people easily, generously and with his whole heart. He modeled living "a life of love" (Ephesians 5:1–2 NIV 1984). Friendship to Jesus was an adventure – wonderful, meaningful and worth everything. Peter was Jesus' friend. Read **John 21:1–22.** What stands out to you as you read this? Much of Peter's training with Jesus was relationship training – how to love God and people well, and why. Imagine for a moment that, like Peter, you're having a relationship training conversation with Jesus over breakfast. How is Jesus inspiring and advising you to experience more genuine, mutual, one-another friendship love in your life? Listen closely. Write down your insights and the scriptures that come to mind. Now go and grow in real love. Pray.

Today: Hear + Practice:

The most excellent way... Love never fails... The greatest of these is love. (1 Corinthians 12:31–13:13)

RESPECT

"Do to others as you would have them do to you." (Luke 6:31)

Most of us want to be treated with kindness and respect, but sometimes we find ourselves caught up in competition and comparison with those around us, resulting in downward cycles of mistrust and fear in our relationships. Amazingly, Jesus rose above those temptations. How did he do it? He drew strength from his Father's and his friends' love and respect for him (love creates a healthy cycle) and found the security and power to genuinely respect and love others. Read **John 4:1–26.** How did Jesus show genuine respect for this woman at the well? How did he connect on a heart level with her? Love is both truthful and tenderhearted. Jesus simply treated her the way he wanted to be treated. Reflect for a moment on how Jesus treated people, and then on how he has treated you. Today, practice respecting all people. Miracles happen when we live the Golden Rule. Pray.

Extra-Strength Exercise: Consider the "love language" of one of your closest friends – what most makes them feel loved. Take a moment this week to express your love to them, in a special way, using their language: words of affirmation, acts of service, gifts, quality time, or physical touch.

Today: Hear + Practice:

Show proper respect to everyone. (1 Peter 2:17)

GRACE & TRUTH

The Word became flesh and made his dwelling among us...full of grace and truth. (John 1:14)

Jesus showed us that building love relationships well requires a wise combination of grace (relational compassion, warmth, favor) and truth (correct information, structure, rules). To Jesus it was not either-or but rather both-and (John 1:14). Read and reflect on **John 8:2–11.** This was a high-pressure scenario. Consider how Jesus thoughtfully and expertly handled it. How did he treat this woman caught in an embarrassing, vulnerable situation? Okay, now think about yourself, your personality – self-awareness is key – do you tend to be more graceful or truthful in your relationships? Remember, both are vital. How is Jesus training you in each of these areas? How has he treated you with both grace and truth? Write down a few insights. Now think of how you can practice a healthy Jesus-balance of grace and truth in a relational interaction that you will have today. Pray.

Today: Hear + Practice:

Jesus said, "If you hold to my teaching, you are really my disciples. Then you will know the truth, and the truth will set you free." (John 8:31–32)

VULNERABILITY

"My soul is overwhelmed with sorrow... Stay here and keep watch with me." (Matthew 26:38)

Jesus needed love from God and others even though it made him vulnerable (susceptible to being wounded or hurt). He embraced his need for others and built relationships of authentic openness, honesty and humility – which, over time, made him strong. He shared his heart, joys, fears, dreams and needs with close friends. He made himself known. He was especially close to three men: Peter, James and John (Matthew 17:1, Mark 1:29–31, Mark 5:37, Mark 14:33, Luke 8:51, John 1:35–42). They spent a lot of time together and faced all kinds of situations. He opened up to them and depended on them. And even though it would cause him great pain, it also gave him greater strength and joy (Hebrews 12:2). Read **Mark 14:26–42** and **14:66–72.** What do you see in Jesus, his realness and vulnerability? How has he been susceptible to being wounded or hurt by you? Who are your friends that you are truly vulnerable with? What are you hearing from Jesus about connecting in true friendship? How will you practice it today? Pray vulnerably.

Today: Hear + Practice:

He took Peter, James and John along with him, and he began to be deeply distressed and troubled. (Mark 14:33)

CHARACTER

"Make a tree good and its fruit will be good, or make a tree bad and its fruit will be bad, for a tree is recognized by its fruit." (Matthew 12:33)

Character is who we are when no one is watching – how we think, feel, believe and behave – our true person. The integrity of our character eventually shows up in our results – who we are on the inside determines our fruit on the outside (Matthew 7:16, 12:33, 23:26). Healthy character builds credibility and trust in relationships. And trust is indispensable in genuinely bonding with one another. While Jesus was a man of strong character, he deeply respected others with strong character and wisdom. Jesus did not rely on shallow appearances, manipulation, facades or popularity to build relationships (John 7:24). Read **Matthew 11:1–19**. What do you learn about character in this passage? What did Jesus mean by saying, "Wisdom is proved right by her deeds"? Write down your insights. Pray for wisdom to practice integrity of character.

Today: Hear + Practice:

"Like a wise man who built his house on the rock..." (Matthew 7:24)

CONVERSATION

...listening to them and asking them questions. (Luke 2:46)

Jesus enjoyed good, hearty conversation. Consider all the conversations Jesus had in the Gospels. From an early age, he learned how to connect with all types of people by actively listening, taking a genuine interest, asking good questions and giving thoughtful responses (Luke 2:46–47). He spoke from his heart and carefully drew out the hearts of others (Proverbs 20:5). Read **John 1:35–51.** What do you learn from a typical day in the life of Jesus about connecting through conversation? How has Jesus cared for, taken a genuine interest in and empathetically listened to you? Today, take an interest in someone, strike up a conversation, and see where it goes. Pray.

Today: Hear + Practice:

The purposes of a person's heart are deep waters, but one who has insight draws them out. (Proverbs 20:5)

FORGIVENESS

"Father, forgive them..." (Luke 23:34)

Forgiveness brings us health and happiness. It frees our hearts to live and love. Conversely, bitterness and unforgiveness make us sick and stuck – prisoners of the past and of the actions of others that we can't control. Jesus holds no grudges, bitterness or resentments. He trusted God and entrusted himself to God (1 Peter 2:23). Incredibly, he forgave and forgives everyone, even those who caused him much pain and suffering – and now he encourages us to do likewise (Mark 11:25). We've all been hurt and sinned against, so God in Christ meets our need for inspiration and training in forgiveness. Read **Luke 7:36–50.** How did forgiveness transform this woman who had "lived a sinful life"? Reflect on how Jesus has forgiven you and how it has changed your life. Read and pray **Luke 11:1–4.** Now go and pass on what you've been given. Enjoy the freedom!

Today: Hear + Practice:

Forgive as the Lord forgave you. (Colossians 3:13)

ONE-ANOTHER LEADERSHIP WORKSHEET

Jesus was intentional about his relationships (with God, friends, family, neighbors, all people). Consider how he built his relationships and imitate his faith and actions.

I. My important relationships:

II. My action steps to faithfully build these relationships:

A friend loves at all times. (Proverbs 17:17)

WEEKLY TRAINING REVIEW

Review and reflect upon what you've learned this week and make solid commitments and clear plans for progress. Then partner with God each day in prayer to become more and more like Jesus (Luke 5:16).

I. My main "Hear + Practice" takeaways from this past week:

II. My training dreams, commitments, plans and prayers:

"...like a man building a house, who dug down deep and laid the foundation on rock." (Luke 6:48)

Week Four

TEAM LEADERSHIP

Love Together

7 Essentials of Winning Teams:

1. **PURPOSE**
2. **PRINCIPLES**
3. **PARTNERSHIPS**
4. **PERSONALITIES**
5. **PRACTICE**
6. **PRAYER**
7. **PEACE**

Jesus enjoyed life with a team of friends – a family. He flourished – lived, loved, trained, served and suffered for and with his team, growing in greatness both individually and together. He needed his team to help him be his best and complete his mission. So do we. Everyone needs a team so they can thrive.

PURPOSE

Jesus...called to him those he wanted... He appointed twelve – designating them apostles. (Mark 3:13–14 NIV 1984)

We all need multiple relationships to fulfill our purpose; no one relationship can meet all our needs – we need a group. Even Jesus didn't go it alone. He accomplished his life's purposes with a team. And he assembled his gang prayerfully and purposefully (Mark 3:13–19, Luke 6:12–16). To fulfill his mission, he needed God, the Spirit, his family, his band of brothers and others – and they needed him and each other. Read **Mark 2:1–13** about a highly successful team. What was their purpose in this situation? How did they rally together to accomplish it? Sometimes we're a mat carrier; sometimes we're on the mat. Who are your mat carriers? Who's helping you to get to Jesus and fulfill your purpose? Who are you helping? Think about your team (whether it's your family, marriage, friends, workplace, growth group…). What is your vision, your mission – your purpose? Write it down. How will you help each other get there? Perhaps today is the day that by "digging through the roof" you make an opening! Pray and practice on purpose..

Today: Hear + Practice:

These twelve Jesus sent out with the following instructions...
(Matthew 10:5)

PRINCIPLES

When Jesus had called the Twelve together, he gave them power and authority. (Luke 9:1)

Every team, family or group has a culture that grows from the practical principles, vision and values of those in the group. Strong and healthy teams are built by consistently hearing and practicing God's word as individuals and together as a team (Luke 8:21). Jesus was proactive and careful to forge a culture in which "unschooled, ordinary" people (Acts 4:13) would become courageous and compassionate people of character – moms, dads, husbands, wives, friends, leaders, disciples, world-changers. Read through **Luke chapter 9.** What are you hearing about how to build a strong culture of faith, commitment, courage, hope and love in your group? Share your insights with someone on your team today and discuss the principles that are guiding your team to mature and to multiply. Pray.

Today: Hear + Practice:

"My mother and brothers are those who hear God's word and put it into practice." (Luke 8:21)

PARTNERSHIPS

Calling the Twelve to him, he began to send them out two by two and gave them authority. (Mark 6:7)

Jesus worked hard to facilitate and forge partnerships among the Twelve. He knew that in just about every area of life we can accomplish more, grow more and become more with a team. But a team (whether it's your family, marriage, kids, friends, neighborhood, workplace group, sports or church) is only as strong as the relationships within it. Strong teams work intentionally to build camaraderie, cooperation and connections among those on the team. These relationships are crucial. Jesus purposefully encouraged deep and real, one-another relationships among the Twelve. Read **Mark 6:1–13.** Here Jesus was facing a low point in his ministry – a lack of faith on the part of his audience. What steps did he take to respond to this challenge personally and with his team? What was the result? Partners empower and encourage each other in times of need. Partner with someone on your team today to overcome and to mutually help each other be your best. Pray together.

Today: Hear + Practice:

Jesus...took Peter, John and James with him and went up onto a mountain to pray. (Luke 9:28)

REVOLUTION

PERSONALITIES

An argument started among the disciples as to which of them would be the greatest. (Luke 9:46)

God created each of us with unique strengths, talents, personalities, perspectives, abilities and opportunities. Jesus recognized, honored and celebrated individuality. His team was made up of twelve unique personalities – all of whom were needed to make the team complete. Read **John 1:35–51** and **Mark 10:35–45.** How did Jesus manage the personalities on his team? We thrive when we are valued for who we are and connect to loving friends who help us to become our best. What are the strengths of those on your team? Take a moment to compliment someone on your team today for what they uniquely bring to your group. Pray.

Extra-Strength Exercise: Write down the names of those in your group or family. Now consider each of their strengths and gifts. Recognize and compliment them for their strengths and consider a special role for each of them in your group or family so their strengths can be optimized.

Today: Hear + Practice:

James and John… Jesus nicknamed them "Sons of Thunder."
(Mark 3:17 NLT)

REVOLUTION

PRACTICE

These twelve Jesus sent out with the following instructions... (Matthew 10:5)

Productive teamwork requires practice. Teams get good at what they practice consistently, building synergy, proficiency and (most important) trust in each other. Great teams are high-trust teams that have invested a lot of time and energy to learn to work as one. Read **Matthew 14:13–36.** How did Jesus and the Twelve practice together? How did Jesus balance team practice with personal practice? Imagine you've just experienced this day in the life of Jesus and the Twelve. What will you take away and practice with your team today? Pray.

Today: Hear + Practice:

When the apostles returned, they reported to Jesus what they had done. (Luke 9:10)

PRAYER

Once when Jesus was praying in private and his disciples were with him... (Luke 9:18)

Consistent prayer is a vital, life-giving practice of healthy families and teams. Jesus worked out regularly with his team in prayer (Luke 9:18, Hebrews 5:7). It made them strong, vibrant and resilient together. Prayer is an essential part of Jesus' training of our heart, soul, mind and body. Prayer plugs us in – connects us to our Almighty God and each other in his transformative, loving, extraordinary power. Prayer is a personal and group conversation with God, vital to building our faith – our understanding of and trust in him. Read **Mark 9:14–29.** What do you think Jesus meant when he said, "This kind can come out only by prayer"? Reflect on this and apply it to your day today. Practice prayer.

Today: Hear + Practice:

They all joined together constantly in prayer. (Acts 1:14)

PEACE

"Peace I leave you; my peace I give you." (John 14:27)

It's an understatement to say that Jesus and his team went through a lot together! Jesus was championship-training his gang to become not merely spectators of a revolution, but to become revolutionaries – healthy, strong-charactered, high-integrity, passionate, bold, global and local peacemakers like Jesus – effective messengers of "good news of great joy…for all the people" (Luke 2:10 ESV). Read **Luke 2:8–14** and **Luke 24:36–53.** The New Testament understanding of "peace" comes from the Hebrew concept of "shalom" meaning "wholeness, health, prosperity." Jesus wants us to live in peace with God and each other (in our family, marriage, friend groups, neighborhood, workplace, church, small group, etc.) and to prosper! What's the next step in your team's peace revolution? Talk about it and take those steps together. Pray.

Today: Hear + Practice:

"I have told you these things, so that in me you may have peace."
(John 16:33)

TEAM LEADERSHIP WORKSHEET

Jesus taught that loving God, one another and our neighbor are the most important priorities in life. Everything good grows from these. Pray, talk together as a group and plan the following:

I. "Love God" – How we will grow in love with God (heart, soul, mind, body):

II. "Love One Another" – How we will grow in love toward one another:

III. "Love Our Neighbor" – How we will grow in love toward our neighbor:

They devoted themselves to the apostles' teaching and to fellowship, to the breaking of bread and to prayer. (Acts 2:42)

WEEKLY TRAINING REVIEW

Review and reflect upon what you've learned this week and make solid commitments and clear plans for progress. Then partner with God each day in prayer to become more and more like Jesus (Luke 5:16).

I. My main "Hear + Practice" takeaways from this past week:

II. My training dreams, commitments, plans and prayers:

"...like a man building a house, who dug down deep and laid the foundation on rock." (Luke 6:48)

Week Five

NEIGHBORHOOD LEADERSHIP

Love Your Neighbor

7 Ways to Share the Love:

1. **SPIRITUAL**
2. **SOCIAL**
3. **SERVING**
4. **SPEAKING**
5. **SEEKING**
6. **SAVING**
7. **SUFFERING**

Jesus was the most effective leader and trainer of leaders in history. His public leadership in the neighborhood, community and workplace inspired and transformed humanity. Now he wants to train each of us how to lead well publicly even in challenging and difficult circumstances.

SPIRITUAL

Jesus returned to Galilee in the power of the Spirit, and news about him spread through the whole countryside. (Luke 4:14)

Jesus taught that if we are to make a positive, lasting impact on the world around us – our neighborhoods, schools, workplaces and communities – we must be spiritually strong and alive on the inside, in our character, as well as among the people. In him was life, and that life was the light of all mankind (John 1:4). He said, "The Spirit gives life; the flesh counts for nothing" (John 6:63). Jesus' Spirit is one of love, joy, peace, forbearance, kindness, goodness, faithfulness, gentleness and self-control (Galatians 5:22–23) – wow, very different from the world around us! This is the Spirit that we receive when we repent and are baptized (Acts 2:38), the Spirit that we get to connect with, walk with, keep in step with – learn to "dance" with – every day. Read **Luke 4:14–37.** How did Jesus activate the incredible power of the Holy Spirit in his life? In addition to prayer, notice the role of God's word. What can you do right now, immediately, to harness the power of the Spirit in your life?

Today: Hear + Practice:

"The Spirit of the Lord is on me, because he has anointed me to proclaim good news to the poor." (Luke 4:18)

SOCIAL

"Here is a glutton and a drunkard, a friend of tax collectors and sinners." (Matthew 11:19)

Jesus was considered by some to be a rebel, a party animal, a friend (what?!) and at times a scandalous socialite because he enjoyed the company of ordinary people outside the circles of the pious and religious elite (Luke 15:1–2). He loved to connect in real life, love and experiences with the tax collectors, drunkards, sinners and overeaters! Jesus valued people more than possessions, relationships more than rules. Read **Mark 2:13–28.** What do you hear Jesus teaching you about connecting more with the world around you (in your school, workplace, community, neighborhood)? How did Jesus reach out to you socially? Reflect on where you were when he called you and where he was willing to go to connect with you. How can you take steps toward being more socially engaged today? Pray to have Jesus' heart.

Extra-Strength Exercise: Think of something you enjoy doing – that "makes you come alive." Now go do that with others in your community.

Today: Hear + Practice:

"Love your neighbor as yourself." (Mark 12:31)

SERVING

"I am among you as one who serves." (Luke 22:27)

Jesus was a person of strong and humble character. He was rooted in God, wisdom, truth, faith, hope and genuine love. He felt loved and served by God Almighty and realized that if God, our Father (Luke 11:2–4) is a servant, and we are not greater than he, then we are called to be servants too – to humbly help others out of simple care and compassion. The truth is, being a servant is how we realize our greatness and help others to realize theirs (Mark 10:21, 35–45, Matthew 25:31–46). Read **Luke 10:25–37.** What do you learn from this encounter? How do we tend to justify ourselves? How has Jesus served you in your time of desperation, when you were left "half dead"? Jesus-like servant leadership changes us and changes the world. How can you step out of your comfort zone and sacrifice for a neighbor today? Pray to notice and care for the needs of others.

Today: Hear + Practice:

"No servant is greater than his master, nor is a messenger greater than the one who sent him." (John 13:16)

SPEAKING

"The words I have spoken to you – they are full of the Spirit and life." (John 6:63)

Someone once said that "our neighborhoods are as open (to the gospel) as our mouths are." It is imperative that we courageously speak up and speak out with words full of the Spirit and life. Jesus spoke life-giving, loving, good and faithful words because the good news was stored up in his heart. He said, "A good man brings good things out of the good stored up in him" (Matthew 12:35). Our neighborhoods need good news spoken, taught, preached and shared with grace and truth. The words we hear, internalize and speak play a huge role in our health and the health of our families, neighborhoods, workplaces and communities. Read **Matthew 12:33–37** and **Matthew 13:1–23.** Think about the power of words. Consider the power of God's words when they take root in our hearts. What words are you hearing from Jesus that you can go and communicate with your neighbor? Sometimes it's simply sharing with others what God has done in our lives (Mark 5:19). Pray to speak the words of Jesus today, words "full of the Spirit and life."

Today: Hear + Practice:

"The mouth speaks what the heart is full of." (Luke 6:45)

SEEKING

"Seek and you will find." (Matthew 7:7)

Jesus was a passionate preacher, teacher, helper and healer "among the people" (Matthew 4:23). He sought to inspire as many as possible – going "through all the towns and villages" (Matthew 9:35) and commissioning his team to "go and make disciples of all nations" (Matthew 28:18–20). Jesus was and is an energetic, genuinely concerned, passionate initiator – he loves to seek and to find (Luke 15). He deeply desires that no one be left for dead, left out or left behind. His mission: search and rescue. And while he gives us room to run our own race, come to our own convictions and seek God in a deeply personal way, he makes himself available, compassionately cares for us and celebrates with exuberant joy when we find our way. Read **Matthew 4:18–25** and **Luke 10:25–37.** To what lengths did Jesus go to seek and find you? Imagine Jesus living in your community or working in your office. How would he love, care for and take an interest in (seek) those around him? Go and do likewise.

Today: Hear + Practice:

"Go and do likewise." (Luke 10:37)

SAVING

"For the Son of Man came to seek and to save the lost." (Luke 19:10)

Just look around – humanity is harassed and helpless (Matthew 9:35–38). Our world desperately needs real hope, light, wisdom and power to help us in our time of need. Jesus cares; he speaks to our real needs – our physical, spiritual, mental and emotional needs. He actively reaches out to us, rescues us and then calls us to care and immediately get involved – to work with urgency, to pitch in, to help, to love and to save our neighbor as we've been helped, loved and saved. Read **Luke 19:1–10.** What do you notice about Jesus' spirit and heart in this encounter with Zacchaeus? How did he reach out and engage with him? Remember some of the meaningful ways in which Jesus and his disciples reached out to you. Be thankful and strive to imitate Jesus' attitude, heart and practice today. Pray to be an effective rescue worker.

Today: Hear + Practice:

"Go into all the world and preach the gospel to all creation."
(Mark 16:15)

SUFFERING

"The Son of Man must suffer many things and be rejected...be killed and...rise again." (Mark 8:31)

To love is to be willing to notice, care for and suffer for others. God loves us so much that he gave us Jesus (John 3:16). Jesus loved us so much that he was willing to "suffer many things" (Mark 8:31) and give his life for us. He is the suffering servant described in the book of Isaiah chapter 53. Read **Mark 5:21–34.** How did Jesus notice this bleeding woman's pain and struggle? How did he respond? In his everyday life, Jesus was willing to be inconvenienced, hurt, opposed, mistreated, fatigued, misunderstood and interrupted for the sake of others. How has he done this for you? Now take a moment to pause and reflect. What are you hearing? Our neighbors need us to be more like Jesus. Pray and consider how you can rise to the challenge.

Today: Hear + Practice:

I want to know Christ – yes, to know the power of his resurrection and participation in his sufferings. (Philippians 3:10)

NEIGHBORHOOD LEADERSHIP WORKSHEET

Jesus loved to share the "good news of great joy…for all the people." He loved his neighbor as himself, treating them the way he wanted to be treated. How would Jesus love your neighbors? Go and do likewise (Luke 10:37).

I. My neighborhoods / My neighbors:

II. My plan to connect with, love and serve my neighbors:

Each of us should please our neighbors for their good, to build them up. (Romans 15:2)

WEEKLY TRAINING REVIEW

Review and reflect upon what you've learned this week and make solid commitments and clear plans for progress. Then partner with God each day in prayer to become more and more like Jesus (Luke 5:16).

I. My main "Hear + Practice" takeaways from this past week:

II. My training dreams, commitments, plans and prayers:

"...like a man building a house, who dug down deep and laid the foundation on rock." (Luke 6:48)

Week Six

SERVANT LEADERSHIP

Love Leaders

7 Leadership Training Principles:

1. **LEAD THE WAY**
2. **HUMBLE SERVICE**
3. **FRIENDSHIP-BASED**
4. **VISION-DRIVEN**
5. **EMPATHETIC LISTENING**
6. **FOLLOW THROUGH**
7. **ENCOURAGEMENT**

Jesus defined leadership as service (Mark 10:35–45). And he multiplied his service impact by multiplying servant leaders. He believed that leaders don't just make followers, they make more leaders (Matthew 28:18–20). Jesus leaders believe in others and help them grow to their full God-given potential.

LEAD THE WAY

They were on their way up to Jerusalem, with Jesus leading the way. (Mark 10:32)

Effective leaders, teachers and coaches lead the way by their example. There's a tongue-in-cheek saying that goes, "Those who can't do, teach." It speaks to our tendency sometimes to hide in our comfort zone, timid and afraid. Jesus is different – he believed, practiced and led the way in what he preached – unlike the hypocrites (Matthew 7:29, Matthew 23). He led the way in vision, courage, compassion, love, humility, action, conviction and sacrifice. His example challenged and inspired other strong-minded men and women to follow, learn and grow. James, the brother of Jesus, warned that being a teacher brings with it responsibility (James 3:1) and that those who strive to teach will be "judged more strictly." The holes in our teaching tend to be the holes in our life. Those we coach and teach will look first to our example. Read **Mark 10:32–34** and **Mark 11:1–18.** What stands out to you from these passages? Write it down. How has Jesus personally led the way for you? How is Jesus training you to be an effective teacher and coach? Pray to walk the talk and lead the way. Then others will be excited to be coached by you.

Today: Hear + Practice:

"Woe to you, teachers of the law and Pharisees, you hypocrites!"
(Matthew 23:15)

HUMBLE SERVICE

"For those who exalt themselves will be humbled, and those who humble themselves will be exalted." (Matthew 23:12)

To become a good trainer, we must first be a good student – an eager, sincere, humble learner from others. How are you leading the way in being trained? Who is actively coaching you? Also, great coaches are genuinely focused on the goals, dreams and growth of those they are training, not on themselves, their own dreams or their own agenda. They've determined to serve, not to be served (Mark 10:45). One of the forces that can hold us back is fear. Jesus served those he was training to grow in character and courage. Read **Luke 5:1–16** and **Acts 4:13.** In the early encounter, how did Jesus inspire and encourage Peter? How did Peter open himself up to be coached? Later, how had others noticed that Peter had grown to become just like Jesus? Now think about someone that you are training to lead. Write down one way that fear is hindering their progress and one way (like Jesus) that you will inspire and encourage (instill courage in) them today. Pray.

Today: Hear + Practice:

He poured water into a basin and began to wash his disciples' feet.
(John 13:5)

FRIENDSHIP-BASED

"You are my friends." (John 15:14)

Effective life, love and leadership coaching is relationship and friendship based. This is how Jesus approached those he was training – as a friend (Luke 7:34, 15:1–2, John 15:13). Jesus sought to connect relationally with those he was coaching to build trust and faith – in a spirit of "we're in this together." Unfortunately, sometimes those we are training will disappoint us and make mistakes – sometimes big ones! Read **Luke 22:1–34.** How did Jesus handle the impending sins and mistakes of Peter and the other apostles? Did he lose faith in them? Did Jesus get resentful, vindictive or controlling, looking down on them? How did he respond? Consider how Jesus has been a compassionate, patient friend to you in your training. Ask yourself if you might be holding anything against those you are training. If so, humbly forgive so that it won't hinder your vision. Pray for those you're training so that their "faith may not fail" (Luke 22:32). Take a minute to express your genuine friendship for and faith in them today. Pray.

Today: Hear + Practice:

They went with James and John to the home of Simon and Andrew.
(Mark 1:29)

VISION-DRIVEN

"You are Simon, John's son – but you shall be called Peter, the rock!" (John 1:42 TLB)

Jesus had a clear vision for his life. He was unstoppable because he knew what he wanted – his vision was vivid, deeply personal and compelling. As an expert coach, he also inspired others to have vision. Jesus believes in all humans (even us!). He knows what we're made of and the greatness we were made for. Jesus defined greatness as excellence of heart, soul, mind and body in loving service of God and people (Mark 10:42–45). And he's the expert on how to overcome both small inconveniences and extreme adversity on the way to realizing our dreams and goals. And while he gives us the room to discover our unique vision – our voice – he also pushes and encourages us out of our comfort zone to dream big. Read **John 5:1–11.** What is your vision for your life? What excuses and mindsets are holding you back? What do you hear from Jesus about having a personal vision and helping others to find theirs? Pray for vision.

Extra-Strength Exercise: Ask someone you're coaching, "What are your dreams and how can I help you realize them?"

Today: Hear + Practice:

Jesus called in a loud voice, "Lazarus, come out!" (John 11:43)

REVOLUTION

EMPATHETIC LISTENING

"Therefore consider carefully how you listen." (Luke 8:18)

Great trainers, teachers and coaches connect emotionally in trust with those whom they are serving. Their students feel understood and known by them, because they ask good questions and genuinely listen, empathize and encourage. Empathy is defined as "the ability to understand and share the feelings of another." Jesus empathizes – relates to us – even sympathizes with our weaknesses (Hebrews 2:10–18). Read **Matthew 16:13–19, 17:24–26** and **John 11:17–44.** What stands out to you in these situations regarding Jesus' training methods? How did he treat each person differently? Why do you think Jesus was "deeply moved in spirit and troubled"? (John 11:33). Consider Jesus' questions and listening in these passages and throughout the Gospels. How has Jesus listened to you personally? Write down a few of your insights. How can you practice Jesus-like asking questions and listening today with someone you are coaching? Pray to connect on a heart level with those you're helping.

Today: Hear + Practice:

"What is written in the Law?... How do you read it?" (Luke 10:26)

REVOLUTION

FOLLOW THROUGH

The apostles gathered around Jesus and reported to him all they had done and taught. (Mark 6:30)

A few essential ingredients in effective coaching are: clear visionary goals and expectations, next-step commitments, positive encouragement and consistent follow-up conversations. We all need these to grow and to help others grow. Jesus demonstrated this powerful coaching pattern in his training relationships. His approach builds relational trust and leads to mutual learning and progress. Read **Mark 6:6–13** and **Mark 6:30–32.** What were the challenges Jesus was facing? How did he respond? What were the results? What stands out to you about Jesus' training pattern? How can you apply these principles and patterns to your training relationships? Pray for clarity and consistency.

Today: Hear + Practice:

**Jesus appeared to his disciples after he was raised from the dead.
(John 21:14)**

ENCOURAGEMENT

"Whoever believes in me...will do even greater things." (John 14:12)

Jesus often gathered with his teammates (individually and in groups) for encouraging pep talks. He understood that losing heart – getting discouraged and negative – could easily lead to defeat. Lack of faith, fear and losing heart are some of the enemy's most effective weapons for keeping our dreams, goals, aspirations, hopes and prayers from coming true. Effective coaches reach those they are training with authentic, encouraging and helpful words that positively facilitate their best thinking, feeling, believing and behaving. The best coaches tend to focus on positive, faithful motivations and the character and personality strengths of those they're coaching. Read **John 14:1–27.** How did Jesus encourage and empower his disciples during this very challenging time? How can you purposefully and positively encourage someone today to overcome fear with faith? Pray for wisdom.

Today: Hear + Practice:

"'If you can'?" said Jesus. "Everything is possible for one who believes." (Mark 9:23)

SERVANT LEADERSHIP WORKSHEET

Jesus was actively involved in helping, coaching, encouraging and teaching others to be their very best. He believed in others and engaged with them in the growth process.

I. Who's training me, and what we're actively working on:

II. Those I'm training – their strengths and weaknesses:

III. Their dreams and goals, and how I'm helping them to achieve them:

Jesus looked at him and loved him. (Mark 10:21)

WEEKLY TRAINING REVIEW

Review and reflect upon what you've learned this week and make solid commitments and clear plans for progress. Then partner with God each day in prayer to become more and more like Jesus (Luke 5:16).

I. My main "Hear + Practice" takeaways from this past week:

II. My training dreams, commitments, plans and prayers:

"...like a man building a house, who dug down deep and laid the foundation on rock." (Luke 6:48)

Week Seven

YOU: JESUS LEADERSHIP

Love Skills

7 Skills of Jesus Leaders:

1. **HUMILITY**
2. **BELIEF**
3. **LOVE**
4. **TEAM**
5. **ACTION**
6. **MULTIPLICATION**
7. **COURAGE**

Jesus taught that we reap what we sow. The skills and habits that we develop shape the person we become and the fruit we bear. When we change our habits of character – our thinking, feeling, believing and acting – we change our whole lives. We must intentionally walk in the way, truth and life of Jesus. Believe. Be fearless. Be the revolution.

HUMILITY

"Only one thing is needed." (Luke 10:42 NIV 1984)

Jesus forged the habit of humility in his own character. He humbled himself before God and people. He made himself nothing, taking the very nature of a servant and became obedient to death – even death on a cross (Philippians 2). He did this for us! He grew strong, gentle and humble in heart. Paradoxically, this one quality of his character – this habit – is the secret to his extraordinary power, impact and success. Humility activates the power of God in our favor (1 Peter 5:5–6, Proverbs 3:34). Jesus was not too proud to listen, learn, surrender, practice and obey (Luke 2:46, John 5:19–23, John 10, Matthew 26:36–46). Now we have an amazing opportunity: we get to sit at his feet to listen and learn, surrender, practice and obey. Read **Luke 10:38–42.** Take a moment to imagine yourself sitting at the Master's feet. What are you feeling? Hearing? Learning? Now consider Jesus' words to you: "Only one thing is needed." What does that mean for you personally, today? Resist the urge to be anxious, proud, dismissive or distracted – "worried and upset about many things." Listen and learn. Practice humility. Pray and choose what is better.

Today: Hear + Practice:

"I am gentle and humble in heart." (Matthew 11:29)

BELIEF

Jesus answered, "The work of God is this: to believe in the one he has sent." (John 6:29)

Belief is powerful and essential to thriving in life, love and leadership. Jesus spoke often of the power of faith, belief and trust (Mark 1:15, Mark 11:22–25, Matthew 9:29, 21:22, John 14:1, 11). He even called belief "the work of God" (John 6:29). Sometimes the promises of God seem so impossible. Sometimes our mission, our dreams, our purpose and our calling seem so challenging! It's hard to conceive of how we could ever realize them. But God knows, and he has the wisdom and the power to do it. And if God has a dream – a mission – for your life (which he does!) he can make it happen in you, through you and with you. Trust God. Seek God. Hear God's voice. Be encouraged. Choose faithful, believing thoughts. Believe in Jesus' training even when it's hard. Put your shoulders back, step up and step out with confidence. Nothing is impossible with God. Read **Luke 1:26–38.** Who was Mary at this moment in her life? What was she feeling? How did the angel advise her? How did Mary respond? Today, practice the simple habit of believing – joyfully trusting, confidently acting in faith. Do the important work of believing, and in God's good time, you will see his promises and blessings come true. Pray. With God all things are possible!

Today: Hear + Practice:

"With man this is impossible, but with God all things are possible." (Matthew 19:26)

LOVE

"A new command I give you." (John 13:34)

Love changes everything for good. It creates a revolutionary, upward, positive, healthy cycle for generations to come. Live a life of love, and you will succeed emotionally, physically, mentally and spiritually. Your family, friends and neighbors will be thankful you did. God is love (1 John 4:16). Love is the most excellent way. Love never fails (1 Corinthians 12:31–13:13). To do what you love, with those you love, for whom you love, because of love is to truly live. God created us to thrive, to flourish, to prosper in life when we live loved, live in love and live to love. Love can be difficult and produce pain in our lives, but the blessings far outweigh the challenges. We make a lot of mistakes when we attempt to love, but love covers over a multitude of sins (1 Peter 4:8). Love pushes us out of our comfort zone to grow and help others grow. Love is Jesus' primary message, his goal, his method and his motivation. Love is Jesus in action – in heart, soul, mind and body. Love is revolutionary. Reread **Mark 12:28–34, Matthew 22:34–40** and **John 13:34–35.** Who are you in love with? Build this habit in your life: hear Jesus' words of love and practice them today. Pray..

Today: Hear + Practice:

And so we know and rely on the love God has for us. God is love. Whoever lives in love lives in God, and God in them. (1 John 4:16)

REVOLUTION

TEAM

After this he went down to Capernaum with his mother and brothers and his disciples. There they stayed for a few days. (John 2:12)

As capable, strong and smart as Jesus was, he didn't take on life by himself – rather, he lived his life with a team. On Jesus' team was God his Father, friends, family and coworkers. And even though they sometimes argued, shifted blame and struggled to get along, the people on his team learned to be faithful to each other, walk with God together, work together for common goals, carry each other's burdens and love one another deeply. Thinking, working, walking and living "team" is a habit that must be practiced regularly and purposefully in order to grow strong. Good teams can accomplish more than great individuals, but they must go through the natural cycles of forming, storming and norming to perform well together. Read **Luke 6:12–16** and **Acts 1:1–14.** Consider the growth path of Jesus' team from when he first called them to when he sent them out to revolutionize the world. What do you learn? How is Jesus training you to be a better teammate and team leader? Today, take steps to practice life as an active part of a loving, faithful team. Pray.

Today: Hear + Practice:

They all joined together constantly in prayer, along with the women and Mary the mother of Jesus, and with his brothers. (Acts 1:14)

ACTION

"Come, follow me...and I will send you out to fish for people." (Mark 1:17)

Taking action is a learned habit. So is procrastination. Jesus teaches us to act boldly. In his teaching style, Jesus was not typically longwinded, meandering or intellectual in his instructions. He was direct, practical and inspirational. He called people to respond with the actions of hearing, believing, doing and persevering. A key to learning is to take practical action on what we've learned – right away! In the Gospels, the words "immediately" and "at once" appear over fifty times. Read **Mark 1:14–20.** Write down a few insights from this passage about taking decisive, positive action (this is "repentance"; see Mark 1:15 and 2 Corinthians 7:10–11). Think about the Gospels and how often Jesus calls people to "go and do" immediately after he instructs them (Matthew 28:19, Mark 5:19, Mark 10:21, Luke 10:3, 37, John 4:16). Why do you think he did this? Write down one important area of your life in which you've been procrastinating. Plan to take one positive action step in this area of your life today. Pray with faithful urgency – now go, do and enjoy!

Extra-Strength Exercise: Talk to your training partner about areas in which each of you tends to procrastinate. Have a good conversation about how you can help each other to proact instead.

Today: Hear + Practice:

"Go and make disciples of all nations, baptizing them... and teaching to obey." (Matthew 28:19–20)

MULTIPLICATION

"Go and make disciples of all nations, baptizing them...and teaching them to obey everything I have commanded you." (Matthew 28:19–20)

One of the secrets of Jesus' extraordinary impact is this: he didn't just manage followers, he multiplied disciples. Even Jesus knew he couldn't do it all himself – he multiplied Jesus leaders, who in turn multiplied more Jesus leaders. Too often those in leadership and caregiving roles limit their impact and burn out because they try to do everything by themselves. Perhaps they feel threatened by others excelling past them. Or perhaps they're too busy doing everything rather than investing the necessary time and heart in careful delegation, teaching, conversation and training. Jesus didn't lead that way. He trusted, encouraged, served and coached others to grow, succeed and lead – even believing that others would do "greater things" than he did (John 14:12). Jesus expected, walked with and helped others to "grow up" – to mature and multiply in faith, hope and love in heart, soul, mind and strength. Multiplying Jesus leaders is a habit that we can develop if we're willing to do it Jesus' way. Read **John 13:1–17.** In this situation, what is Jesus teaching you? What are you hearing, observing and learning from him? How will you pass it on? How must you die to multiply? How will you, like Jesus, train others to grow by your service, faith and enthusiasm? Pray to become effective in multiplying the faith, hope and love of Jesus in others.

Today: Hear + Practice:

"I have set you an example that you should do as I have done for you." (John 13:15)

COURAGE

Jesus told him, "Don't be afraid; just believe." (Mark 5:36)

Faith, courage, trust and belief are powerful, enabling us to move mountains. When we believe, we find the strength to persevere despite adversity and hardship, all the way to the finish. Courage and belief are like muscles: they must be developed and strengthened with training. Read **Mark 5:21–43.** In this tense situation, Jesus encouraged others with a simple statement: "Don't be afraid; just believe." And because he believed, he was able to move forward. He then courageously comforted this twelve-year-old girl and her family with tender compassion, empathetic connection and positive faith. Consider how Jesus has knelt down, taken your hand and spoken words of faith into your life. What do you hear Jesus specifically teaching you about courage from this passage? Okay, now consider your challenges. How have fear, anxiety and worry been stopping you? Pause and envision how you will courageously choose to *"just believe"* and keep moving forward. God instructs us with the words, "Don't be afraid" about 365 times in the Bible – one for every day, including today. Pray, just believe, then continue on (God's got your back!).

Today: Hear + Practice:

When they saw the courage of Peter and John and realized that they were unschooled, ordinary men, they were astonished, and they took note that these men had been with Jesus. (Acts 4:13)

YOU: JESUS LEADER WORKSHEET

Jesus gives us the necessary training, spirit and structure in our relationships to build new habits and character in our lives. To do this, we must replace existing character patterns with new ways of thinking, feeling, believing and behaving. Talk to God and have some conversations with friends – then consider and commit to the following:

I. Existing patterns in my life that I need and want to change:

II. New patterns that I will choose and train daily with Jesus and others:

But solid food is for the mature, who by constant use have trained themselves to distinguish good from evil. (Hebrews 5:14)

7-WEEKLY TRAINING REVIEW

Review and reflect upon what you've learned this week and make solid commitments and clear plans for progress. Then partner with God each day in prayer to become more and more like Jesus (Luke 5:16).

I. My main "Hear + Practice" takeaways from this past week:

II. My training dreams, commitments, plans and prayers:

"...like a man building a house, who dug down deep and laid the foundation on rock." (Luke 6:48)

REVOLUTIONARY HABIT

"If you remain in me and my words remain in you..." – Jesus (John 15)

One Simple Revolutionary Habit:
Train with Jesus every day
Hear + Practice = Thrive

I. How I've grown:

II. How I will continue to hear, practice, train and build on the Rock:

GOOD NEWS

"...good news of great joy...for all the people" (Luke 2:10 ESV)

Wait, there's more! Jesus generously gives us all the good stuff we need for personal and public revolution. Fifty days after Jesus' resurrection, Peter – a changed man because of the training and love of Jesus – stood up courageously before thousands from the surrounding nations to preach the gospel message – good news of great joy for all people. The revolution had already been sparked in the hearts and lives of those on Jesus' team and his small community of revolutionaries. Now they were taking it to the streets and would eventually take it to the ends of the earth. Peter spoke boldly about getting a brand-new start in life and love with God, one another and our neighbor. He taught about hearing and practicing Jesus' words. Read **Matthew 28:18–20, Acts 1:1–8** and **Acts 2:36–47.** What are you hearing about true revolution? Have you repented and been baptized in the name of Jesus Christ for the forgiveness of your sins and to receive the Holy Spirit? Have you shared this revolution with others? How will you let the fire and faith of the first-century fighters inspire your revolution? Pray, go and do likewise.

Those who accepted his message were baptized, and about three thousand were added to their number that day. They devoted themselves to the apostles' teaching and to the fellowship, to the breaking of bread and to prayer. (Acts 2:41–42)